Harlem Shadows

Harlem Shadows
Claude McKay

MINT EDITIONS

Harlem Shadows was first published in 1922.

This edition published by Mint Editions 2021.

ISBN 9781513299341 | E-ISBN 9781513224060

Published by Mint Editions®

MINT
EDITIONS

minteditionbooks.com

Publishing Director: Jennifer Newens
Design & Production: Rachel Lopez Metzger
Project Manager: Micaela Clark
Typesetting: Westchester Publishing Services

Introduction

These poems have a special interest for all the races of man because they are sung by a pure blooded Negro. They are the first significant expression of that race in poetry. We tried faithfully to give a position in our literature to Paul Laurence Dunbar. We have excessively welcomed other black poets of minor talent, seeking in their music some distinctive quality other than the fact that they wrote it. But here for the first time we find our literature vividly enriched by a voice from this most alien race among us. And it should be illuminating to observe that while these poems are characteristic of that race as we most admire it—they are gentle-simple, candid, brave and friendly, quick of laughter and of tears—yet they are still more characteristic of what is deep and universal in mankind. There is no special or exotic kind of merit in them, no quality that demands a transmutation of our own natures to perceive. Just as the sculptures and wood and ivory carvings of the vast forgotten African Empires of Ifé and Benin, although so wistful in their tranquility are tranquil in the possession of the qualities of all classic and great art, so these poems, the purest of them, move with a sovereignty that is never new to the lovers of the high music of human utterance.

It is the peculiarity of his experience, rather than of his nature, that makes this poet's race a fact to be remembered in the enjoyment of his songs. The subject of all poetry is the experience of the poet, and no man of any other race in the world can touch or imagine the experience of the children of African slaves in America.

Claude McKay was born in 1890 in a little thatched house of two rooms in a beautiful valley of the hilly middle-country of Jamaica. He was born to the genial, warm, patient, neighborly farmer's life of that island. It was a life rich in sun and sound and color and emotion, as we can see in his poems which are forever homeward yearning—in the midst of their present passion and strong will into the future, forever vividly remembering. Like a blue-bird's note in a March wind, those sudden clear thoughts of the warm South ring out in the midst of his northern songs. They carry a thrill into the depth of our hearts. Perhaps in some sense they are thoughts of a mother. At least it seems inevitable that we should find among them those two sacred sonnets of a child's bereavement. It seems inevitable that a wonderful poet should have had a wise and beautiful mother.

We can only distantly imagine how the happy tropic life of play and affection, became shadowed and somber for this sensitive boy as he grew, by a sense of the subjection of his people, and the memory of their bondage to an alien race. Indeed the memory of Claude McKay's family goes back on his mother's side beyond the days of bondage, to a time in Madagascar when they were still free, and by the grace of God still "savage." He learned in early childhood the story of their violent abduction, and how they were freighted over the seas in ships, and sold at public auction in Jamaica. He learned another story, too, which must have kindled a fire that slept in his blood—a story of the rebellion of the members of his own family at the auction-block. A death-strike, we should call it now—for they agreed that if they were divided and sold away into different parts of the country they would all kill themselves. And this fact solemnly announced in the market by the oldest white-haired Negro among them, had such an effect upon prospective buyers that it was impossible to sell them as individuals, and so they were all taken away together to those hills at Clarendon which their descendants still cultivate. With the blood of these rebels in his veins, and their memory to stir it, we cannot wonder that Claude McKay's earliest boyish songs in the Jamaica dialect were full of heresy and the militant love of freedom, and that his first poem of political significance should have been a rally-call to the street-car men on strike in Kingston. He found himself by an instinctive gravitation singing in the forefront of the battle for human liberty. A wider experience and a man's comprehension of the science of history has only strengthened his voice and his resolution.

Those early songs and the music he composed for them, were very popular in Jamaica. Claude McKay was quite the literary prince of the island for a time—a kind of Robert Burns among his own people, as we can imagine, with his physical beauty, his quick sympathy, and the magnetic wayward humor of his ways. He received in 1912 the medal of the Institute of Arts and Sciences in recognition of his preëminence. He was the first Negro to receive this medal, and he was the first poet who ever made songs in the quaint haunting dialect of the island. But nevertheless it was not until he came to the United States that Claude McKay began to confront the deepest feelings in his heart, and realize that a delicate syllabic music could not alone express them. Here his imagination awoke, and the colored imagery that is the language of all deep passion began to appear in his poetry. Here too he conceived and felt the history and position of his people with mature poetic force. He knew that his voice belonged not only to his own moods and the general experience of humanity, but to the hopes and sorrows of his race.

A great many foolish things are said even by wise people upon the subject of racial inferiority. They seem to think that if science could establish a certain difference of average ability as between the whites and blacks, that would justify them in placing the whole of one of these races in a position of inferior esteem. The same fallacy is committed in the discussions of sex-inferiority, and it is worth-while to make clear the perfect folly of it. If any defined quantitative difference is ever established between the average abilities of such groups, it will be a relatively slight one. The difficulty of establishing it, is a proof of that. And a slight difference in the general average would have no application whatever as between any two individuals, or any minor groups of individuals. The enormous majority of both races, as of both sexes, would show the same degree of ability. And so great is the factor of individual variation that we could not even be sure an example of the highest ability might not arise in the group whose average was "inferior." This simple consideration of fact and good logic should suffice to silence those who think they can ever appeal to science in support of a general race or sex prejudice.

But in so far as the problem arises between a dominant and a subjected race, it is impossible for science to say anything even as to averages. For a fair general test is impossible. The children of the subjected race never have a chance. To be deprived at the very dawn of selfhood of a sense of possible superiority, is to be undernourished at the point of chief educative importance. And to be assailed in early childhood with a pervading intimation of inferiority is poison in the very centers of growth. Except for people of the highest force of character, therefore, to be born into a subjected race is to grow up inferior, not only to the other race, but to one's own potential self. We see an example of this kind of growth in the bombastic locutions of the traditional "darkie" who has acquired a little culture. Those great big words and long sentences are the result of a feeling of inferiority. They are a pathetic over-correction of the very quality of simple-heartedness which is carried so high in these poems of Claude McKay. It is carried so high, and made so boldly beautiful, that we cannot withhold a tribute to his will, as well as to his music and imagination. The naked force of character that we feel in those two recent sonnets, "Baptism" and "The White City," is no mere verbal semblance. Its reality is certified by the very achievement of such commanding art in the face of a contemptuous or condescending civilization.

Claude McKay came to the United States in 1912, having been offered an education here by a friend in Jamaica who believed in his abilities. His intention was to learn scientific farming, and return to the island to offer practical wisdom as well as music to his people. He went at first to one of our established philanthropic institutions for the training of colored people. He stayed there a few months—long enough to weary of the almost military system of discipline. And then he went to the Agricultural College of Kansas, where he had learned that a free life and a more elective system of education prevailed. He studied for two years there, thinking continually less about farming and more about literature, and gradually losing away altogether the idea of returning to live in Jamaica. He left the college in 1914, knowing that he was a poet—and imagining, I think, that he was a rather irresponsible and wayward character—to cast in his lot with the working-class Negroes of the north. Since then he has earned his living in every one of the ways that the northern Negroes do, from "pot-wrestling" in a boarding-house kitchen to dining-car service on the New York and Philadelphia Express. But like all true poets, he failed to take the duty of "earning a living" very seriously. It was a matter of collecting enough money from each new job to quit for a while and live. And with each period of living a new and a more sure and beautiful song would come out of him.

The growth of beauty and sureness in these songs would be apparent if they were arranged in the order of their creation. As it is, the reader will observe occasional lapses of quality. One or two of the rhythms I confess I am not able to apprehend at all. Perhaps they will be picked up by receivers who are attuned to a different wavelength. But the quality is here in them all—the pure, clear arrow-like transference of his emotion into our breast, without any but the inevitable words—the quality that reminds us of Burns and Villon and Catullus, and all the poets that we call lyric because we love them so much. It is the quality that Keats sought to cherish when he said that "Poetry should be great and unobtrusive, a thing which enters into the soul, and does not startle or amaze with itself but with its subject." Poetry with this quality is not for those whose interest is mainly in the manufacture of poems. It will come rather to those whose interest is in the life of things. It is the poetry of life, and not of the poet's chamber. It is the poetry that looks upon a thing, and sings. It is possessed by a feeling and sings. May it find its way a little quietly and softly, in this age of roar and advertising, to the hearts that love a true and unaffected song.

Max Eastman

Author's Word

In putting ideas and feelings into poetry, I have tried in each case to use the medium most adaptable to the specific purpose. I own allegiance to no master. I have never found it possible to accept in entirety any one poet. But I have loved and joyed in what I consider the finest in the poets of all ages.

The speech of my childhood and early youth was the Jamaica Negro dialect, the native variant of English, which still preserves a few words of African origin, and which is more difficult of understanding than the American Negro dialect. But the language we wrote and read in school was England's English. Our textbooks then, before the advent of the American and Jamaican readers and our teachers, too, were all English-made. The native teachers of the elementary schools were tutored by men and women of British import. I quite remember making up verses in the dialect and in English for our moonlight ring dances and for our school parties. Of our purely native songs the jammas (field and road), shay-shays (yard and booth), wakes (post-mortem), Anancy tales (transplanted African folk lore), and revivals (religious) are all singularly punctuated by meter and rhyme. And nearly all my own poetic thought has always run naturally into these regular forms.

Consequently, although very conscious of the new criticisms and trends in poetry, to which I am keenly responsive and receptive, I have adhered to such of the older traditions as I find adequate for my most lawless and revolutionary passions and moods. I have not used patterns, images and words that would stamp me a classicist nor a modernist. My intellect is not scientific enough to range me on the side of either; nor, is my knowledge wide enough for me to specialize in any school.

I have never studied poetics; but the forms I have used I am convinced are the ones I can work in with the highest degree of spontaneity and freedom.

I have chosen my melodies and rhythms by instinct, and I have favored words and figures which flow smoothly and harmoniously into my compositions. And in all my moods I have striven to achieve directness, truthfulness and naturalness of expression instead of an enameled originality. I have not hesitated to use words which are old, and in some circles considered poetically overworked and dead, when I thought I could make them glow alive by new manipulation. Nor have

I stinted my senses of the pleasure of using the decorative metaphor where it is more truly and vividly beautiful than the exact phrase. But for me there is more quiet delight in "The golden moon of heaven" than in "The terra-cotta disc of cloud-land."

Finally, while I have welcomed criticism, friendly and unfriendly, and listened with willing attention to many varying opinions concerning other poems and my own, I have always, in the summing up, fallen back on my own ear and taste as the arbiter.

Claude McKay

THE EASTER FLOWER

Far from this foreign Easter damp and chilly
    My soul steals to a pear-shaped plot of ground,
Where gleamed the lilac-tinted Easter lily
    Soft-scented in the air for yards around;

Alone, without a hint of guardian leaf!
    Just like a fragile bell of silver rime,
It burst the tomb for freedom sweet and brief
    In the young pregnant year at Eastertime;

And many thought it was a sacred sign,
    And some called it the resurrection flower;
And I, a pagan, worshiped at its shrine,
    Yielding my heart unto its perfumed power.

To One Coming North

At first you'll joy to see the playful snow,
    Like white moths trembling on the tropic air,
Or waters of the hills that softly flow
    Gracefully falling down a shining stair.

And when the fields and streets are covered white
    And the wind-worried void is chilly, raw,
Or underneath a spell of heat and light
    The cheerless frozen spots begin to thaw,

Like me you'll long for home, where birds' glad song
    Means flowering lanes and leas and spaces dry,
And tender thoughts and feelings fine and strong,
    Beneath a vivid silver-flecked blue sky.

But oh! more than the changeless southern isles,
    When Spring has shed upon the earth her charm,
You'll love the Northland wreathed in golden smiles
    By the miraculous sun turned glad and warm.

America

Although she feeds me bread of bitterness,
And sinks into my throat her tiger's tooth,
Stealing my breath of life, I will confess
I love this cultured hell that tests my youth!
Her vigor flows like tides into my blood,
Giving me strength erect against her hate.
Her bigness sweeps my being like a flood.
Yet as a rebel fronts a king in state,
I stand within her walls with not a shred
Of terror, malice, not a word of jeer.
Darkly I gaze into the days ahead,
And see her might and granite wonders there,
Beneath the touch of Time's unerring hand,
Like priceless treasures sinking in the sand.

Alfonso, Dressing to Wait at Table

Alfonso is a handsome bronze-hued lad
    Of subtly-changing and surprising parts;
His moods are storms that frighten and make glad,
    His eyes were made to capture women's hearts.

Down in the glory-hole Alfonso sings
    An olden song of wine and clinking glasses
And riotous rakes; magnificently flings
    Gay kisses to imaginary lasses.

Alfonso's voice of mellow music thrills
    Our swaying forms and steals our hearts with joy;
And when he soars, his fine falsetto trills
    Are rarest notes of gold without alloy.

But, O Alfonso! wherefore do you sing
    Dream-songs of carefree men and ancient places?
Soon we shall be beset by clamoring
    Of hungry and importunate palefaces.

THE TROPICS IN NEW YORK

Bananas ripe and green, and ginger-root,
    Cocoa in pods and alligator pears,
And tangerines and mangoes and grapefruit,
    Fit for the highest prize at parish fairs,

Set in the window, bringing memories
    Of fruit-trees laden by low-singing rills,
And dewy dawns, and mystical blue skies
    In benediction over nun-like hills.

My eyes grew dim, and I could no more gaze;
    A wave of longing through my body swept,
And, hungry for the old, familiar ways,
    I turned aside and bowed my head and wept.

Flame-Heart

So much have I forgotten in ten years,
  So much in ten brief years! I have forgot
What time the purple apples come to juice,
  And what month brings the shy forget-me-not.
I have forgot the special, startling season
  Of the pimento's flowering and fruiting;
What time of year the ground doves brown the fields
  And fill the noonday with their curious fluting.
I have forgotten much, but still remember
The poinsettia's red, blood-red in warm December.

I still recall the honey-fever grass,
  But cannot recollect the high days when
We rooted them out of the ping-wing path
  To stop the mad bees in the rabbit pen.
I often try to think in what sweet month
  The languid painted ladies used to dapple
The yellow by-road mazing from the main,
  Sweet with the golden threads of the rose-apple.
I have forgotten strange but quite remember
The poinsettia's red, blood-red in warm December.

What weeks, what months, what time of the mild year
  We cheated school to have our fling at tops?
What days our wine-thrilled bodies pulsed with joy
  Feasting upon blackberries in the copse?
Oh some I know! I have embalmed the days,
  Even the sacred moments when we played,
All innocent of passion, uncorrupt,
  At noon and evening in the flame-heart's shade.
We were so happy, happy, I remember,
Beneath the poinsettia's red in warm December.

HOME THOUGHTS

Oh something just now must be happening there!
That suddenly and quiveringly here,
Amid the city's noises, I must think
Of mangoes leaning o'er the river's brink,
And dexterous Davie climbing high above,
The gold fruits ebon-speckled to remove,
And toss them quickly in the tangled mass
Of wis-wistwisted round the guinea grass;
And Cyril coming through the bramble-track
A prize bunch of bananas on his back;
And Georgie—none could ever dive like him—
Throwing his scanty clothes off for a swim;
And schoolboys, from Bridge-tunnel going home,
Watching the waters downward dash and foam.
This is no daytime dream, there's something in it,
Oh something's happening there this very minute!

On Broadway

About me young and careless feet
Linger along the garish street;
  Above, a hundred shouting signs
Shed down their bright fantastic glow
  Upon the merry crowd and lines
Of moving carriages below.
Oh wonderful is Broadway—only
My heart, my heart is lonely.

Desire naked, linked with Passion,
Goes strutting by in brazen fashion;
  From playhouse, cabaret and inn
The rainbow lights of Broadway blaze
  All gay without, all glad within;
As in a dream I stand and gaze
At Broadway, shining Broadway—only
My heart, my heart is lonely.

The Barrier

I must not gaze at them although
    Your eyes are dawning day;
I must not watch you as you go
    Your sun-illumined way;

I hear but I must never heed
    The fascinating note,
Which, fluting like a river reed,
    Comes from your trembling throat;

I must not see upon your face
    Love's softly glowing spark;
For there's the barrier of race,
    You're fair and I am dark.

Adolescence

There was a time when in late afternoon
    The four-o'clocks would fold up at day's close
Pink-white in prayer, and 'neath the floating moon
    I lay with them in calm and sweet repose.

And in the open spaces I could sleep,
    Half-naked to the shining worlds above;
Peace came with sleep and sleep was long and deep,
    Gained without effort, sweet like early love.

But now no balm—nor drug nor weed nor wine—
    Can bring true rest to cool my body's fever,
Nor sweeten in my mouth the acid brine,
    That salts my choicest drink and will forever.

Homing Swallows

Swift swallows sailing from the Spanish main,
    O rain-birds racing merrily away
From hill-tops parched with heat and sultry plain
    Of wilting plants and fainting flowers, say—

When at the noon-hour from the chapel school
    The children dash and scamper down the dale,
Scornful of teacher's rod and binding rule
    Forever broken and without avail,

Do they still stop beneath the giant tree
    To gather locusts in their childish greed,
And chuckle when they break the pods to see
    The golden powder clustered round the seed?

THE CITY'S LOVE

For one brief golden moment rare like wine,
The gracious city swept across the line;
Oblivious of the color of my skin,
Forgetting that I was an alien guest,
She bent to me, my hostile heart to win,
Caught me in passion to her pillowy breast;
The great, proud city, seized with a strange love,
Bowed down for one flame hour my pride to prove.

North and South

O sweet are tropic lands for waking dreams!
    There time and life move lazily along.
There by the banks of blue-and-silver streams
    Grass-sheltered crickets chirp incessant song,
Gay-colored lizards loll all through the day,
    Their tongues outstretched for careless little flies,
And swarthy children in the fields at play,
    Look upward laughing at the smiling skies.
A breath of idleness is in the air
    That casts a subtle spell upon all things,
And love and mating-time are everywhere,
    And wonder to life's commonplaces clings.
The fluttering humming-bird darts through the trees
    And dips his long beak in the big bell-flowers,
The leisured buzzard floats upon the breeze,
    Riding a crescent cloud for endless hours,
The sea beats softly on the emerald strands—
O sweet for quiet dreams are tropic lands!

WILD MAY

Aleta mentions in her tender letters,
Among a chain of quaint and touching things,
That you are feeble, weighted down with fetters,
And given to strange deeds and mutterings.
No longer without trace or thought of fear,
Do you leap to and ride the rebel roan
But have become the victim of grim care,
With three brown beauties to support alone.
But none the less will you be in my mind,
Wild May that cantered by the risky ways,
With showy head-cloth flirting in the wind,
From market in the glad December days;
Wild May of whom even other girls could rave
Before sex tamed your spirit, made you slave.

The Plateau

It was the silver, heart-enveloping view
    Of the mysterious sea-line far away,
    Seen only on a gleaming gold-white day,
That made it dear and beautiful to you.

And Laura loved it for the little hill,
    Where the quartz sparkled fire, barren and dun,
    Whence in the shadow of the dying sun,
She contemplated Hallow's wooden mill.

While Danny liked the sheltering high grass,
    In which he lay upon a clear dry night,
    To hear and see, screened skillfully from sight,
The happy lovers of the valley pass.

But oh! I loved it for the big round moon
    That swung out of the clouds and swooned aloft,
    Burning with passion, gloriously soft,
Lighting the purple flowers of fragrant June.

AFTER THE WINTER

Someday, when trees have shed their leaves
    And against the morning's white
The shivering birds beneath the eaves
    Have sheltered for the night,
We'll turn our faces southward, love,
    Toward the summer isle
Where bamboos spire to shafted grove
    And wide-mouthed orchids smile.

And we will seek the quiet hill
    Where towers the cotton tree,
And leaps the laughing crystal rill,
    And works the droning bee.
And we will build a cottage there
    Beside an open glade,
With black-ribbed blue-bells blowing near,
    And ferns that never fade.

THE WILD GOAT

O you would clothe me in silken frocks
    And house me from the cold,
And bind with bright bands my glossy locks,
    And buy me chains of gold;

And give me—meekly to do my will—
    The hapless sons of men:—
But the wild goat bounding on the barren hill
    Droops in the grassy pen.

Harlem Shadows

I hear the halting footsteps of a lass
    In Negro Harlem when the night lets fall
Its veil. I see the shapes of girls who pass
    To bend and barter at desire's call.
Ah, little dark girls who in slippered feet
Go prowling through the night from street to street!

Through the long night until the silver break
    Of day the little gray feet know no rest;
Through the lone night until the last snow-flake
    Has dropped from heaven upon the earth's white breast,
The dusky, half-clad girls of tired feet
Are trudging, thinly shod, from street to street.

Ah, stern harsh world, that in the wretched way
    Of poverty, dishonor and disgrace,
Has pushed the timid little feet of clay,
    The sacred brown feet of my fallen race!
Ah, heart of me, the weary, weary feet
In Harlem wandering from street to street.

THE WHITE CITY

I will not toy with it nor bend an inch.
Deep in the secret chambers of my heart
I muse my life-long hate, and without flinch
I bear it nobly as I live my part.
My being would be a skeleton, a shell,
If this dark Passion that fills my every mood,
And makes my heaven in the white world's hell,
Did not forever feed me vital blood.
I see the mighty city through a mist—
The strident trains that speed the goaded mass,
The poles and spires and towers vapor-kissed,
The fortressed port through which the great ships pass,
The tides, the wharves, the dens I contemplate,
Are sweet like wanton loves because I hate.

THE SPANISH NEEDLE

Lovely dainty Spanish needle
    With your yellow flower and white,
Dew bedecked and softly sleeping,
    Do you think of me tonight?

Shadowed by the spreading mango,
    Nodding o'er the rippling stream,
Tell me, dear plant of my childhood,
    Do you of the exile dream?

Do you see me by the brook's side
    Catching crayfish 'neath the stone,
As you did the day you whispered:
    Leave the harmless dears alone?

Do you see me in the meadow
    Coming from the woodland spring
With a bamboo on my shoulder
    And a pail slung from a string?

Do you see me all expectant
    Lying in an orange grove,
While the swee-swees sing above me,
    Waiting for my elf-eyed love?

Lovely dainty Spanish needle,
    Source to me of sweet delight,
In your far-off sunny southland
    Do you dream of me tonight?

MY MOTHER

I

Reg wished me to go with him to the field,
I paused because I did not want to go;
But in her quiet way she made me yield
Reluctantly, for she was breathing low.
Her hand she slowly lifted from her lap
And, smiling sadly in the old sweet way,
She pointed to the nail where hung my cap.
Her eyes said: I shall last another day.
But scarcely had we reached the distant place,
When o'er the hills we heard a faint bell ringing;
A boy came running up with frightened face;
We knew the fatal news that he was bringing.
I heard him listlessly, without a moan,
Although the only one I loved was gone.

II

The dawn departs, the morning is begun,
The trades come whispering from off the seas,
The fields of corn are golden in the sun,
The dark-brown tassels fluttering in the breeze;
The bell is sounding and the children pass,
Frog-leaping, skipping, shouting, laughing shrill,
Down the red road, over the pasture-grass,
Up to the schoolhouse crumbling on the hill.
The older folk are at their peaceful toil,
Some pulling up the weeds, some plucking corn,
And others breaking up the sunbaked soil.
Float, faintly-scented breeze, at early morn
Over the earth where mortals sow and reap—
Beneath its breast my mother lies asleep.

In Bondage

I would be wandering in distant fields
Where man, and bird, and beast, lives leisurely,
And the old earth is kind, and ever yields
Her goodly gifts to all her children free;
Where life is fairer, lighter, less demanding,
And boys and girls have time and space for play
Before they come to years of understanding—
Somewhere I would be singing, far away.
For life is greater than the thousand wars
Men wage for it in their insatiate lust,
And will remain like the eternal stars,
When all that shines today is drift and dust
But I am bound with you in your mean graves,
O black men, simple slaves of ruthless slaves.

December, 1919

Last night I heard your voice, mother,
    The words you sang to me
When I, a little barefoot boy,
    Knelt down against your knee.

And tears gushed from my heart, mother,
    And passed beyond its wall,
But though the fountain reached my throat
    The drops refused to fall.

'Tis ten years since you died, mother,
    Just ten dark years of pain,
And oh, I only wish that I
    Could weep just once again.

HERITAGE

Now the dead past seems vividly alive,
    And in this shining moment I can trace,
Down through the vista of the vanished years,
    Your faun-like form, your fond elusive face.

And suddenly some secret spring's released,
    And unawares a riddle is revealed,
And I can read like large, black-lettered print,
    What seemed before a thing forever sealed.

I know the magic word, the graceful thought,
    The song that fills me in my lucid hours,
The spirit's wine that thrills my body through,
    And makes me music-drunk, are yours, all yours.

I cannot praise, for you have passed from praise,
    I have no tinted thoughts to paint you true;
But I can feel and I can write the word;
    The best of me is but the least of you.

WHEN I HAVE PASSED AWAY

When I have passed away and am forgotten,
    And no one living can recall my face,
When under alien sod my bones lie rotten
    With not a tree or stone to mark the place;

Perchance a pensive youth, with passion burning,
    For olden verse that smacks of love and wine,
The musty pages of old volumes turning,
    May light upon a little song of mine,

And he may softly hum the tune and wonder
    Who wrote the verses in the long ago;
Or he may sit him down awhile to ponder
    Upon the simple words that touch him so.

Enslaved

Oh when I think of my long-suffering race,
For weary centuries despised, oppressed,
Enslaved and lynched, denied a human place
In the great life line of the Christian West;
And in the Black Land disinherited,
Robbed in the ancient country of its birth,
My heart grows sick with hate, becomes as lead,
For this my race that has no home on earth.
Then from the dark depths of my soul I cry
To the avenging angel to consume
The white man's world of wonders utterly:
Let it be swallowed up in earth's vast womb,
Or upward roll as sacrificial smoke
To liberate my people from its yoke!

I Shall Return

I shall return again; I shall return
To laugh and love and watch with wonder-eyes
At golden noon the forest fires burn,
Wafting their blue-black smoke to sapphire skies.
I shall return to loiter by the streams
That bathe the brown blades of the bending grasses,
And realize once more my thousand dreams
Of waters rushing down the mountain passes.
I shall return to hear the fiddle and fife
Of village dances, dear delicious tunes
That stir the hidden depths of native life,
Stray melodies of dim remembered runes.
I shall return, I shall return again,
To ease my mind of long, long years of pain.

Morning Joy

At night the wide and level stretch of wold,
Which at high noon had basked in quiet gold,
Far as the eye could see was ghostly white;
Dark was the night save for the snow's weird light.

I drew the shades far down, crept into bed;
Hearing the cold wind moaning overhead
Through the sad pines, my soul, catching its pain,
Went sorrowing with it across the plain.

At dawn, behold! the pall of night was gone,
Save where a few shrubs melancholy, lone,
Detained a fragile shadow. Golden-lipped
The laughing grasses heaven's sweet wine sipped.

The sun rose smiling o'er the river's breast,
And my soul, by his happy spirit blest,
Soared like a bird to greet him in the sky,
And drew out of his heart Eternity.

Africa

The sun sought thy dim bed and brought forth light,
The sciences were sucklings at thy breast;
When all the world was young in pregnant night
Thy slaves toiled at thy monumental best.
Thou ancient treasure-land, thou modern prize,
New peoples marvel at thy pyramids!
The years roll on, thy sphinx of riddle eyes
Watches the mad world with immobile lids.
The Hebrews humbled them at Pharaoh's name.
Cradle of Power! Yet all things were in vain!
Honor and Glory, Arrogance and Fame!
They went. The darkness swallowed thee again.
Thou art the harlot, now thy time is done,
Of all the mighty nations of the sun.

On a Primitive Canoe

Here, passing lonely down this quiet lane,
Before a mud-splashed window long I pause
To gaze and gaze, while through my active brain
Still thoughts are stirred to wakefulness; because
Long, long ago in a dim unknown land,
A massive forest-tree, ax-felled, adze-hewn,
Was deftly done by cunning mortal hand
Into a symbol of the tender moon.
Why does it thrill more than the handsome boat
That bore me o'er the wild Atlantic ways,
And fill me with rare sense of things remote
From this harsh life of fretful nights and days?
I cannot answer but, whate'er it be,
An old wine has intoxicated me.

Winter in the Country

Sweet life! how lovely to be here
    And feel the soft sea-laden breeze
Strike my flushed face, the spruce's fair
    Free limbs to see, the lesser trees'

Bare hands to touch, the sparrow's cheep
    To heed, and watch his nimble flight
Above the short brown grass asleep.
    Love glorious in his friendly might,

Music that every heart could bless,
    And thoughts of life serene, divine,
Beyond my power to express,
    Crowd round this lifted heart of mine!

But oh! to leave this paradise
    For the city's dirty basement room,
Where, beauty hidden from the eyes,
    A table, bed, bureau and broom

In corner set, two crippled chairs
    All covered up with dust and grim
With hideousness and scars of years,
    And gaslight burning weird and dim,

Will welcome me. . . And yet, and yet
    This very wind, the winter birds,

The glory of the soft sunset,
    Come there to me in words.

To Winter

Stay, season of calm love and soulful snows!
There is a subtle sweetness in the sun,
The ripples on the stream's breast gaily run,
The wind more boisterously by me blows,
And each succeeding day now longer grows.
The birds a gladder music have begun,
The squirrel, full of mischief and of fun,
From maples' topmost branch the brown twig throws.
I read these pregnant signs, know what they mean:
I know that thou art making ready to go.
Oh stay! I fled a land where fields are green
Always, and palms wave gently to and fro,
And winds are balmy, blue brooks ever sheen,
To ease my heart of its impassioned woe.

Spring in New Hampshire

(To J. L. J. F. E.)

Too green the springing April grass,
　　Too blue the silver-speckled sky,
For me to linger here, alas,
　　While happy winds go laughing by,
Wasting the golden hours indoors,
Washing windows and scrubbing floors.

Too wonderful the April night,
　　Too faintly sweet the first May flowers,
The stars too gloriously bright,
　　For me to spend the evening hours,
When fields are fresh and streams are leaping,
Wearied, exhausted, dully sleeping.

On the Road

Roar of the rushing train fearfully rocking,
Impatient people jammed in line for food,
The rasping noise of cars together knocking,
And worried waiters, some in ugly mood,
Crowding into the choking pantry hole
To call out dishes for each angry glutton
Exasperated grown beyond control,
From waiting for his soup or fish or mutton.
At last the station's reached, the engine stops;
For bags and wraps the red-caps circle round;
From off the step the passenger lightly hops,
And seeks his cab or tram-car homeward bound:
The waiters pass out weary, listless, glum,
To spend their tips on harlots, cards and rum.

The Harlem Dancer

Applauding youths laughed with young prostitutes
And watched her perfect, half-clothed body sway;
Her voice was like the sound of blended flutes
Blown by black players upon a picnic day.
She sang and danced on gracefully and calm,
The light gauze hanging loose about her form;
To me she seemed a proudly-swaying palm
Grown lovelier for passing through a storm.
Upon her swarthy neck black shiny curls
Luxuriant fell; and tossing coins in praise,
The wine-flushed, bold-eyed boys, and even the girls,
Devoured her shape with eager, passionate gaze;
But looking at her falsely-smiling face,
I knew her self was not in that strange place.

DAWN IN NEW YORK

The Dawn! The Dawn! The crimson-tinted, comes
Out of the low still skies, over the hills,
Manhattan's roofs and spires and cheerless domes!
The Dawn! My spirit to its spirit thrills.
Almost the mighty city is asleep,
No pushing crowd, no tramping, tramping feet.
But here and there a few cars groaning, creep
Along, above, and underneath the street,
Bearing their strangely-ghostly burdens by,
The women and the men of garish nights,
Their eyes wine-weakened and their clothes awry,
Grotesques beneath the strong electric lights.
The shadows wane. The Dawn comes to New York.
And I go darkly-rebel to my work.

The Tired Worker

O whisper, O my soul! The afternoon
Is waning into evening, whisper soft!
Peace, O my rebel heart! for soon the moon
From out its misty veil will swing aloft!
Be patient, weary body, soon the night
Will wrap thee gently in her sable sheet,
And with a leaden sigh thou wilt invite
To rest thy tired hands and aching feet.
The wretched day was theirs, the night is mine;
Come tender sleep, and fold me to thy breast.
But what steals out the gray clouds red like wine?
O dawn! O dreaded dawn! O let me rest
Weary my veins, my brain, my life! Have pity!
No! Once again the harsh, the ugly city.

Outcast

For the dim regions whence my fathers came
My spirit, bondaged by the body, longs.
Words felt, but never heard, my lips would frame;
My soul would sing forgotten jungle songs.
I would go back to darkness and to peace,
But the great western world holds me in fee,
And I may never hope for full release
While to its alien gods I bend my knee.
Something in me is lost, forever lost,
Some vital thing has gone out of my heart,
And I must walk the way of life a ghost
Among the sons of earth, a thing apart;
For I was born, far from my native clime,
Under the white man's menace, out of time.

I Know My Soul

I plucked my soul out of its secret place,
And held it to the mirror of my eye,
To see it like a star against the sky,
A twitching body quivering in space,
A spark of passion shining on my face.
And I explored it to determine why
This awful key to my infinity
Conspires to rob me of sweet joy and grace.
And if the sign may not be fully read,
If I can comprehend but not control,
I need not gloom my days with futile dread,
Because I see a part and not the whole.
Contemplating the strange, I'm comforted
By this narcotic thought: I know my soul.

Birds of Prey

Their shadow dims the sunshine of our day,
As they go lumbering across the sky,
Squawking in joy of feeling safe on high,
Beating their heavy wings of owlish gray.
They scare the singing birds of earth away
As, greed-impelled, they circle threateningly,
Watching the toilers with malignant eye,
From their exclusive haven—birds of prey.
They swoop down for the spoil in certain might,
And fasten in our bleeding flesh their claws.
They beat us to surrender weak with fright,
And tugging and tearing without let or pause,
They flap their hideous wings in grim delight,
And stuff our gory hearts into their maws.

The Castaways

The vivid grass with visible delight
Springing triumphant from the pregnant earth,
The butterflies, and sparrows in brief flight
Chirping and dancing for the season's birth,
The dandelions and rare daffodils
That touch the deep-stirred heart with hands of gold,
The thrushes sending forth their joyous trills,—
Not these, not these did I at first behold!
But seated on the benches daubed with green,
The castaways of life, a few asleep,
Some withered women desolate and mean,
And over all, life's shadows dark and deep.
Moaning I turned away, for misery
I have the strength to bear but not to see.

Exhortation: Summer, 1919

Through the pregnant universe rumbles life's terrific thunder,
And Earth's bowels quake with terror; strange and terrible storms break,
Lightning-torches flame the heavens, kindling souls of men, thereunder:
Africa! long ages sleeping, O my motherland, awake!

In the East the clouds glow crimson with the new dawn that is breaking,
And its golden glory fills the western skies.
O my brothers and my sisters, wake! arise!
For the new birth rends the old earth and the very dead are waking,
Ghosts are turned flesh, throwing off the grave's disguise,
And the foolish, even children, are made wise;
For the big earth groans in travail for the strong, new world in making—
O my brothers, dreaming for dim centuries,
Wake from sleeping; to the East turn, turn your eyes!

Oh the night is sweet for sleeping, but the shining day's for working;
Sons of the seductive night, for your children's children's sake,
From the deep primeval forests where the crouching leopard's lurking,
Lift your heavy-lidded eyes, Ethiopia! awake!

In the East the clouds glow crimson with the new dawn that is breaking,
And its golden glory fills the western skies.
O my brothers and my sisters, wake! arise!
For the new birth rends the old earth and the very dead are waking,
Ghosts are turned flesh, throwing off the grave's disguise,
And the foolish, even children, are made wise;
For the big earth groans in travail for the strong, new world in making—
O my brothers, dreaming for long centuries,
Wake from sleeping; to the East turn, turn your eyes!

CLAUDE MCKAY

The Lynching

His Spirit in smoke ascended to high heaven.
His father, by the cruelest way of pain,
Had bidden him to his bosom once again;
The awful sin remained still unforgiven.
All night a bright and solitary star
(Perchance the one that ever guided him,
Yet gave him up at last to Fate's wild whim)
Hung pitifully o'er the swinging char.
Day dawned, and soon the mixed crowds came to view
The ghastly body swaying in the sun
The women thronged to look, but never a one
Showed sorrow in her eyes of steely blue;
And little lads, lynchers that were to be,
Danced round the dreadful thing in fiendish glee.

Baptism

Into the furnace let me go alone;
Stay you without in terror of the heat.
I will go naked in for thus 'tis sweet
Into the weird depths of the hottest zone.
I will not quiver in the frailest bone,
You will not note a flicker of defeat;
My heart shall tremble not its fate to meet,
My mouth give utterance to any moan.
The yawning oven spits forth fiery spears;
Red aspish tongues shout wordlessly my name.
Desire destroys, consumes my mortal fears,
Transforming me into a shape of flame.
I will come out, back to your world of tears,
A stronger soul within a finer frame.

If We Must Die

If we must die, let it not be like hogs
Hunted and penned in an inglorious spot,
While round us bark the mad and hungry dogs,
Making their mock at our occurs lot.
If we must die, O let us nobly die,
So that our precious blood may not be shed
In vain; then even the monsters we defy
Shall be constrained to honor us though dead!
O kinsmen! we must meet the common foe!
Though far outnumbered let us show us brave,
And for their thousand blows deal one death-blow!
What though before us lies the open grave?
Like men we'll face the murderous, cowardly pack,
Pressed to the wall, dying, but fighting back!

Subway Wind

Far down, down through the city's great, gaunt Gut
The gray train rushing bears the weary wind;
In the packed cars the fans the crowd's breath cut,
 Leaving the sick and heavy air behind.
And pale-cheeked children seek the upper door
 To give their summer jackets to the breeze;
Their laugh is swallowed in the deafening roar
 Of captive wind that moans for fields and seas;
Seas cooling warm where native schooners drift
 Through sleepy waters, while gulls wheel and sweep,
Waiting for windy waves the keels to lift
 Lightly among the islands of the deep;
Islands of lofty palm trees blooming white
 That lend their perfume to the tropic sea,
Where fields lie idle in the dew drenched night,
 And the Trades float above them fresh and free.

THE NIGHT FIRE

No engines shrieking rescue storm the night,
And hose and hydrant cannot here avail;
The flames laugh high and fling their challenging light,
And clouds turn gray and black from silver-pale.
The fire leaps out and licks the ancient walls,
And the big building bends and twists and groans.
A bar drops from its place; a rafter falls
Burning the flowers. The wind in frenzy moans.
The watchers gaze, held wondering by the fire,
The dwellers cry their sorrow to the crowd,
The flames beyond themselves rise higher, higher,
To lose their glory in the frowning cloud,
Yielding at length the last reluctant breath.
And where life lay asleep broods darkly death.

POETRY

Sometimes I tremble like a storm-swept flower,
And seek to hide my tortured soul from thee.
Bowing my head in deep humility
Before the silent thunder of thy power.
Sometimes I flee before thy blazing light,
As from the specter of pursuing death;
Intimidated lest thy mighty breath,
Windways, will sweep me into utter night.
For oh, I fear they will be swallowed up—
The loves which are to me of vital worth,
My passion and my pleasure in the earth—
And lost forever in thy magic cup!
I fear, I fear my truly human heart
Will perish on the altar-stone of art!

To a Poet

There is a lovely noise about your name,
    Above the shoutings of the city clear,
More than a moment's merriment, whose claim
    Will greater grow with every mellowed year.

The people will not bear you down the street,
    Dancing to the strong rhythm of your words,
The modern kings will throttle you to greet
    The piping voice of artificial birds.

But the rare lonely spirits, even mine,
    Who love the immortal music of all days,
Will see the glory of your trailing line,
    The bedded beauty of your haunting lays.

A Prayer

'Mid the discordant noises of the day I hear thee calling;
I stumble as I fare along Earth's way; keep me from falling.

Mine eyes are open but they cannot see for gloom of night;
I can no more than lift my heart to thee for inward light.

The wild and fiery passion of my youth consumes my soul;
In agony I turn to thee for truth and self-control.

For Passion and all the pleasures it can give will die the death;
But this of me eternally must live, thy borrowed breath.

'Mid the discordant noises of the day I hear thee calling;
I stumble as I fare along Earth's way; keep me from falling.

When Dawn Comes to the City

The tired cars go grumbling by,
    The moaning, groaning cars,
And the old milk carts go rumbling by
    Under the same dull stars.
Out of the tenements, cold as stone,
    Dark figures start for work;
I watch them sadly shuffle on,
      'Tis dawn, dawn in New York.

But I would be on the island of the sea,
    In the heart of the island of the sea,
Where the cocks are crowing, crowing, crowing,
    And the hens are cackling in the rose-apple tree,
Where the old draft-horse is neighing, neighing, neighing
    Out on the brown dew-silvered lawn,
    And the tethered cow is lowing, lowing, lowing,
And dear old Ned is braying, braying, braying,
And the shaggy Nannie goat is calling, calling, calling

From her little trampled corner of the long wide lea
That stretches to the waters of the hill-stream Falling
Sheer upon the flat rocks joyously!
    There, oh there! on the island of the sea,
      There I would be at dawn.

The tired cars go grumbling by,
      The crazy, lazy cars,
And the same milk carts go rumbling by
      Under the dying stars.
A lonely newsboy hurries by,
      Humming a recent ditty;
Red streaks strike through the gray of the sky,
      The dawn comes to the city.

But I would be on the island of the sea,
In the heart of the island of the sea,
Where the cocks are crowing, crowing, crowing,
And the hens are cackling in the rose-apple tree,
Where the old draft-horse is neighing, neighing, Neighing
Out on the brown dew-silvered lawn,
And the tethered cow is lowing, lowing, lowing,
And dear old Ned is braying, braying, braying,
And the shaggy Nannie goat is calling, calling, calling
From her little trampled corner of the long wide lea
That stretches to the waters of the hill-stream falling
    Sheer upon the flat rocks joyously!
    There, oh there! on the island of the sea,
        There I would be at dawn.

O Word I Love To Sing

O word I love to sing! thou art too tender
    For all the passions agitating me;
For all my bitterness thou art too tender,
    I cannot pour my red soul into thee.

O haunting melody! thou art too slender,
    Too fragile like a globe of crystal glass;
For all my stormy thoughts thou art too slender,
    The burden from my bosom will not pass.

O tender word! O melody so slender!
    O tears of passion saturate with brine,
O words, unwilling words, ye cannot render
    My hatred for the foe of me and mine.

Absence

Your words dropped into my heart like pebbles into a pool,
Rippling around my breast and leaving it melting cool.

Your kisses fell sharp on my flesh like dawn-dews from the limb,
Of a fruit-filled lemon tree when the day is young and dim.

Like soft rain-christened sunshine, as fragile as rare gold lace,
Your breath, sweet-scented and warm, has kindled my tranquil face.

But a silence vasty-deep, oh deeper than all these ties
Now, through the menacing miles, brooding between us lies.

And more than the songs I sing, I await your written word,
To stir my fluent blood as never your presence stirred.

Summer Morn in New Hampshire

All yesterday it poured, and all night long
    I could not sleep; the rain unceasing beat
Upon the shingled roof like a weird song,
    Upon the grass like running children's feet.
And down the mountains by the dark cloud kissed,
    Like a strange shape in filmy veiling dressed,
Slid slowly, silently, the wraith-like mist,
    And nestled soft against the earth's wet breast.

But lo, there was a miracle at dawn!
    The still air stirred at touch of the faint breeze,
The sun a sheet of gold bequeathed the lawn,
    The songsters twittered in the rustling trees.
And all things were transfigured in the day,
    But me whom radiant beauty could not move;
For you, more wonderful, were far away,
    And I was blind with hunger for your love.

Rest in Peace

No more for you the city's thorny ways,
 The ugly corners of the Negro belt;
The miseries and pains of these harsh days
 By you will never, never again be felt.

No more, if still you wander, will you meet
 With nights of unabating bitterness;
They cannot reach you in your safe retreat,
 The city's hate, the city's prejudice!

'Twas sudden—but your menial task is done,
 The dawn now breaks on you, the dark is over,
The sea is crossed, the longed-for port is won;
 Farewell, oh, fare you well! my friend and lover.

A Red Flower

Your lips are like a southern lily red,
    Wet with the soft rain-kisses of the night,
In which the brown bee buries deep its head,
    When still the dawn's a silver sea of light.

Your lips betray the secret of your soul,
    The dark delicious essence that is you,
A mystery of life, the flaming goal
    I seek through mazy pathways strange and new.

Your lips are the red symbol of a dream.
    What visions of warm lilies they impart,
That line the green bank of a fair blue stream,
    With butterflies and bees close to each heart!

Brown bees that murmur sounds of music rare,
    That softly fall upon the languorous breeze,
Wafting them gently on the quiet air
    Among untended avenues of trees.

O were I hovering, a bee, to probe
    Deep down within your scented heart, fair flower,
Enfolded by your soft vermilion robe,
    Amorous of sweets, for but one perfect hour!

COURAGE

O lonely heart so timid of approach,
    Like the shy tropic flower that shuts its lips
    To the faint touch of tender finger tips:
What is your word? What question would you broach?

Your lustrous-warm eyes are too sadly kind
    To mask the meaning of your dreamy tale,
    Your guarded life too exquisitely frail
Against the daggers of my warring mind.

There is no part of the unyielding earth,
    Even bare rocks where the eagles build their nest,
    Will give us undisturbed and friendly rest.
No dewfall softens this vast belt of dearth.

But in the socket-chiseled teeth of strife,
    That gleam in serried files in all the lands,
    We may join hungry, understanding hands,
And drink our share of ardent love and life.

To O.E.A.

Your voice is the color of a robin's breast,
    And there's a sweet sob in it like rain still rain in the night.
Among the leaves of the trumpet-tree, close to his nest,
    The pea-dove sings, and each note thrills me with strange delight
Like the words, wet with music, that well from your trembling throat.
    I'm afraid of your eyes, they're so bold,
    Searching me through, reading my thoughts, shining like gold.
But sometimes they are gentle and soft like the dew on the lips of the
        eucharis
Before the sun comes warm with his lover's kiss.
    You are sea-foam, pure with the star's loveliness,
Not mortal, a flower, a fairy, too fair for the beauty-shorn earth.
All wonderful things, all beautiful things, gave of their wealth to
        your birth.
    Oh I love you so much, not recking of passion, that I feel it is wrong!
    But men will love you, flower, fairy, non-mortal spirit
            burdened with flesh,
    Forever, life-long.

ROMANCE

To clasp you now and feel your head close-pressed,
Scented and warm against my beating breast;

To whisper soft and quivering your name,
And drink the passion burning in your frame;

To lie at full length, taut, with cheek to cheek,
And tease your mouth with kisses till you speak

Love words, mad words, dream words, sweet senseless words,
Melodious like notes of mating birds;

To hear you ask if I shall love always,
And myself answer: Till the end of days;

To feel your easeful sigh of happiness
When on your trembling lips I murmur: Yes;

It is so sweet. We know it is not true.
What matters it? The night must shed her dew.

We know it is not true, but it is sweet—
The poem with this music is complete.

FLOWER OF LOVE

The perfume of your body dulls my sense.
    I want nor wine nor weed; your breath alone
Suffices. In this moment rare and tense
    I worship at your breast. The flower is blown,
The saffron petals tempt my amorous mouth,
    The yellow heart is radiant now with dew
Soft-scented, redolent of my loved South;
    O flower of love! I give myself to you.
Uncovered on your couch of figured green,
    Here let us linger indivisible.
The portals of your sanctuary unseen
    Receive my offering, yielding unto me.
Oh, with our love the night is warm and deep!
    The air is sweet, my flower, and sweet the flute
Whose music lulls our burning brain to sleep,
    While we lie loving, passionate and mute.

THE SNOW FAIRY

I

Throughout the afternoon I watched them there,
Snow-fairies falling, falling from the sky,
Whirling fantastic in the misty air,
Contending fierce for space supremacy.
And they flew down a mightier force at night,
As though in heaven there was revolt and riot,
And they, frail things had taken panic flight
Down to the calm earth seeking peace and quiet.
I went to bed and rose at early dawn
To see them huddled together in a heap,
Each merged into the other upon the lawn,
Worn out by the sharp struggle, fast asleep.
The sun shone brightly on them half the day,
By night they stealthily had stol'n away.

II

And suddenly my thoughts then turned to you
Who came to me upon a winter's night,
When snow-sprites round my attic window flew,
Your hair disheveled, eyes aglow with light.
My heart was like the weather when you came,
The wanton winds were blowing loud and long;
But you, with joy and passion all aflame,
You danced and sang a lilting summer song.
I made room for you in my little bed,
Took covers from the closet fresh and warm,
A downful pillow for your scented head,
And lay down with you resting in my arm.
You went with Dawn. You left me ere the day,
The lonely actor of a dreamy play.

La Paloma in London

About Soho we went before the light;
We went, unresting six, craving new fun,
New scenes, new raptures, for the fevered night
Of rollicking laughter, drink and song, was done.
The vault was void, but for the dawn's great star
That shed upon our path its silver flame,
When La Paloma on a low guitar
Abruptly from a darkened casement came—
Harlem! All else shut out, I saw the hall,
And you in your red shoulder sash come dancing
With Val against me languid by the wall,
Your burning coffee-colored eyes keen glancing
Aslant at mine, proud in your golden glory!
I loved you, Cuban girl, fond sweet Diory.

A Memory of June

When June comes dancing o'er the death of May,
  With scarlet roses tinting her green breast,
And mating thrushes ushering in her day,
  And Earth on tiptoe for her golden guest,

I always see the evening when we met—
  The first of June baptized in tender rain
And walked home through the wide streets, gleaming wet,
  Arms locked, our warm flesh pulsing with love's pain.

I always see the cheerful little room,
  And in the corner, fresh and white, the bed,
Sweet scented with a delicate perfume,
  Wherein for one night only we were wed;

Where in the starlit stillness we lay mute,
  And heard the whispering showers all night long,
And your brown burning body was a lute
  Whereon my passion played his fevered song.

When June comes dancing o'er the death of May,
  With scarlet roses staining her fair feet,
My soul takes leave of me to sing all day
  A love so fugitive and so complete.

FLIRTATION

Upon thy purple mat thy body bare
    Is fine and limber like a tender tree.
The motion of thy supple form is rare,
    Like a lithe panther lolling languidly,
Toying and turning slowly in her lair.
    Oh, I would never ask for more of thee,
Thou art so clean in passion and so fair.
    Enough! if thou wilt ask no more of me!

TORMENTED

I will not reason, wrestle here with you,
    Though you pursue and worry me about;
As well put forth my swarthy arm to stop
    The wild wind howling, darkly mad without.

The night is yours for revels; day will light.
    I will not fight you, bold and tigerish,
For I am weak, while you are gaining strength;
    Peace! cease tormenting me to have your wish.

But when you're filled and sated with the flesh,
    I shall go swiftly to the silver stream,
To cleanse my body for the spirit's sake,
    And sun my limbs, and close my eyes to dream.

POLARITY

Nay, why reproach each other, be unkind,
    For there's no plane on which we two may meet?
Let's both forgive, forget, for both were blind,
    And life is of a day, and time is fleet.

And I am fire, swift to flame and burn,
    Melting with elements high overhead,
While you are water in an earthly urn,
    All pure, but heavy, and of hue like lead.

One Year After

I

Not once in all our days of poignant love,
Did I a single instant give to thee
My undivided being wholly free.
Not all thy potent passion could remove
The barrier that loomed between to prove
The full supreme surrendering of me.
Oh, I was beaten, helpless utterly
Against the shadow-fact with which I strove.
For when a cruel power forced me to face
The truth which poisoned our illicit wine,
That even I was faithless to my race
Bleeding beneath the iron hand of thine,
Our union seemed a monstrous thing and base!
I was an outcast from thy world and mine.

II

Adventure-seasoned and storm-buffeted,
I shun all signs of anchorage, because
The zest of life exceeds the bound of laws.
New gales of tropic fury round my head
Break lashing me through hours of soulful dread;
But when the terror thins and, spent, withdraws,
Leaving me wondering awhile, I pause—
But soon again the risky ways I tread!
No rigid road for me, no peace, no rest,
While molten elements run through my blood;
And beauty-burning bodies manifest
Their warm, heart-melting motions to be wooed;
And passion boldly rising in my breast,
Like rivers of the Spring, lets loose its flood.

French Leave

No servile little fear shall daunt my will
    This morning. I have courage steeled to say
I will be lazy, conqueringly still,
    I will not lose the hours in toil this day.

The roaring world without, careless of souls,
    Shall leave me to my placid dream of rest,
My four walls shield me from its shouting ghouls,
    And all its hates have fled my quiet breast.

And I will loll here resting, wide awake,
    Dead to the world of work, the world of love,
I laze contented just for dreaming's sake
    With not the slightest urge to think or move.

How tired unto death, how tired I was!
    Now for a day I put my burdens by,
And like a child amidst the meadow grass
    Under the southern sun, I languid lie

And feel the bed about me kindly deep,
    My strength ooze gently from my hollow bones,
My worried brain drift aimlessly to sleep,
    Like softening to a song of tuneful tones.

JASMINES

Your scent is in the room.
Swiftly it overwhelms and conquers me!
Jasmines, night jasmines, perfect of perfume,
Heavy with dew before the dawn of day!
Your face was in the mirror. I could see
You smile and vanish suddenly away,
Leaving behind the vestige of a tear.
Sad suffering face, from parting grown so dear!
Night jasmines cannot bloom in this cold place;
Without the street is wet and weird with snow;
The cold nude trees are tossing to and fro;
Too stormy is the night for your fond face;
For your low voice too loud the wind's mad roar.
But oh, your scent is here—jasmines that grow
Luxuriant, clustered round your cottage door!

COMMEMORATION

When first your glory shone upon my face
    My body kindled to a mighty flame,
And burnt you yielding in my hot embrace
    Until you swooned to love, breathing my name.

And wonder came and filled our night of sleep,
    Like a new comet crimsoning the sky;
And stillness like the stillness of the deep
    Suspended lay as an unuttered sigh.

I never again shall feel your warm heart flushed,
    Panting with passion, naked unto mine,
Until the throbbing world around is hushed
    To quiet worship at our scented shrine.

Nor will your glory seek my swarthy face,
    To kindle and to change my jaded frame
Into a miracle of godlike grace,
    Transfigured, bathed in your immortal flame.

MEMORIAL

Your body was a sacred cell always,
    A jewel that grew dull in garish light,
An opal which beneath my wondering gaze
    Gleamed rarely, softly throbbing in the night.

I touched your flesh with reverential hands,
    For you were sweet and timid like a flower
That blossoms out of barren tropic sands,
    Shedding its perfume in one golden hour.

You yielded to my touch with gentle grace,
    And though my passion was a mighty wave
That buried you beneath its strong embrace,
    You were yet happy in the moment's grave.

Still more than passion consummate to me,
    More than the nuptials immemorial sung,
Was the warm thrill that melted me to see
    Your clean brown body, beautiful and young;

The joy in your maturity at length,
    The peace that filled my soul like cooling wine,
When you responded to my tender strength,
    And pressed your heart exulting into mine.

How shall I with such memories of you
    In coarser forms of love fruition find?
No, I would rather like a ghost pursue
    The fairy phantoms of my lonely mind.

THIRST

My spirit wails for water, water now!
My tongue is aching dry, my throat is hot
For water, fresh rain shaken from a bough,
Or dawn dews heavy in some leafy spot.
My hungry body's burning for a swim
In sunlit water where the air is cool,
As in Trout Valley where upon a limb
The golden finch sings sweetly to the pool.
Oh water, water, when the night is done,
When day steals gray-white through the
    window-pane,
Clear silver water when I wake, alone,
All impotent of parts, of fevered brain;
Pure water from a forest fountain first,
To wash me, cleanse me, and to quench my thirst!

FUTILITY

Oh, I have tried to laugh the pain away,
Let new flames brush my love-springs like a feather.
But the old fever seizes me today,
As sickness grips a soul in wretched weather.
I have given up myself to every urge,
With not a care of precious powers spent,
Have bared my body to the strangest scourge,
To soothe and deaden my heart's unhealing rent.
But you have torn a nerve out of my frame,
A gut that no physician can replace,
And reft my life of happiness and aim.
Oh what new purpose shall I now embrace?
What substance hold, what lovely form pursue,
When my thought burns through everything to you?

THROUGH AGONY

I

All night, through the eternity of night,
Pain was my portion though I could not feel.
Deep in my humbled heart you ground your heel,
Till I was reft of even my inner light,
Till reason from my mind had taken flight,
And all my world went whirling in a reel.
And all my swarthy strength turned cold like steel,
A passive mass beneath your puny might.
Last night I gave you triumph over me,
So I should be myself as once before,
I marveled at your shallow mystery,
And haunted hungrily your temple door.
I gave you sum and substance to be free,
Oh, you shall never triumph any more!

II

I do not fear to face the fact and say,
How darkly-dull my living hours have grown,
My wounded heart sinks heavier than stone,
Because I loved you longer than a day!
I do not shame to turn myself away
From beckoning flowers beautifully blown,
To mourn your vivid memory alone
In mountain fastnesses austerely gray.
The mists will shroud me on the utter height,
The salty, brimming waters of my breast
Will mingle with the fresh dews of the night
To bathe my spirit hankering to rest.
But after sleep I'll wake with greater might,
Once more to venture on the eternal quest.

A Note About the Author

Claude McKay (1889–1948) was a Jamaican poet and novelist. Born in Sunny Ville, Jamaica, McKay was raised in a strict Baptist family alongside seven siblings. Sent to live with his brother Theo, a journalist, at the age of nine, McKay excelled in school while reading poetry in his free time. In 1912, he published his debut collection *Songs of Jamaica*, the first poems written in Jamaican Patois to appear in print. That same year, he moved to the United States to attend the Tuskegee Institute, though he eventually transferred to Kansas State University. Upon his arrival in the South, he was shocked by the racism and segregation experienced by Black Americans, which—combined with his reading of W. E. B. Du Bois' work—inspired him to write political poems and to explore the principles of socialism. He moved to New York in 1914 without completing his degree, turning his efforts to publishing poems in *The Seven Arts* and later *The Liberator*, where he would serve as co-executive editor from 1919 to 1922. Over the next decade, he would devote himself to communism and black radicalism, joining the Industrial Workers of the World, opposing the efforts of Marcus Garvey and the NAACP, and travelling to Britain and Russia to meet with communists and write articles for various leftist publications. McKay, a bisexual man, was also a major figure of the Harlem Renaissance, penning *Harlem Shadows* (1922), a successful collection of poems, and *Home to Harlem* (1928), an award-winning novel exploring Harlem's legendary nightlife.

A Note from the Publisher

Spanning many genres, from non-fiction essays to literature classics to children's books and lyric poetry, Mint Edition books showcase the master works of our time in a modern new package. The text is freshly typeset, is clean and easy to read, and features a new note about the author in each volume. Many books also include exclusive new introductory material. Every book boasts a striking new cover, which makes it as appropriate for collecting as it is for gift giving. Mint Edition books are only printed when a reader orders them, so natural resources are not wasted. We're proud that our books are never manufactured in excess and exist only in the exact quantity they need to be read and enjoyed.

Discover more of your favorite classics with Bookfinity™.

- Track your reading with custom book lists.
- Get great book recommendations for your personalized Reader Type.
- Add reviews for your favorite books.
- AND MUCH MORE!

Visit **bookfinity.com** and take the fun Reader Type quiz to get started.

Enjoy our classic and modern companion pairings!

Printed in the USA
CPSIA information can be obtained
at www.ICGtesting.com
JSHW080005150824
68134JS00021B/2292